For Sandra,
with lots of
Good memories

Myrtle
1995

Artists in Adobe

Artists in Adobe

By Myrtle Stedman

Santa Fe
New Mexico

On the cover: Watercolor, 1934, by Myrtle Stedman
Courtesy of the Wendy Hill Collection

First edition

Printed in the United States of America

Library of Congress Cataloging in Publication Data

Stedman, Myrtle.
        Artists in adobe / by Myrtle Stedman. -- 1st ed.
           p.   cm.
        ISBN 0-86534-188-5 : $8.95
        1. Stedman, Myrtle. 2. Stedman, Wilfred, 1892-1950
        3. Architects--New Mexico--Santa Fe-Biography. I. Title.
        NA737 .S637A2 1993
        720' .92--dc20
        [B]   92-32659
                                       CIP

Published by Sunstone Press
            Post Office Box 2321
            Santa Fe, New Mexico 87504-2321 / USA

Dedicated to
Daddies and Mommies,
Little ones,
Granddaddies
and
Grandmommies
everywhere.

Introduction

This is a sing-a-long,
    ding-a-long story
        which begins—

Once upon a time in
nineteen twenty-nine,
the year the banks
went bust in America,
there were two big-city artists
whose careers involved
architecture too.

Her name was Myrtle.
His name was Wilfred.

They lived in a studio home they designed and built where people loved to come to see their art work— and their house.

But there was suddenly
no art work selling
and no building going on.
This made the two artists
superconscious of the
fire engines at night
and of ambulances
and police that
made so much noise
they could not sleep.

On Sunday they went to
the bay where their
two children could play
and the artists could
sit and dream of
an adobe house in
a quiet little old town
called Santa Fe.

So Wilfred, in their own
back yard, made a house
of mud and clay to
entertain the boys
and the black maid;
and to convince himself
of what he was about to do.

Then he got in his car
and said goodbye to Myrtle,
the boys, and the maid . . .

. . . and drove . . .

through the oil fields

and through the country
where an Indian sat
on his horse . . .

. . . and through the mountains
into a valley on the
north fringe of Santa Fe,
New Mexico.

And in this valley of Tesuque
he bought a fruit ranch
from a very tired old man—

and with the ranch came
the old man's chickens,
pigs and goats.

Back he went
to the city . . .

. . . to pack up . . .

and say goodbye,
then take his little family
off to "God's Country,"

where several artists of
like mind already lived.

At the ranch,

Myrtle took one look and cried.

There were sticks and
stones, broken bottles,
tin cans and a
complete mess of
old and flying paper
everywhere.

Wilfred told Myrtle,
"We will make this place
so beautiful you will
never want to leave it."

The house was an
adobe ruin, but in it
was an old black stove,
a barrel for a table
and kerosene lamps.

Myrtle cried again
and baby Wilfred too;
their organized home
was miles and miles
or years and
years away.

But they cleaned up
the yard, Wilfred and
"Number One Boy,"
Tommie. And
"Number Two Boy"
helped scrub up the house.

They had no telephone,
no electricity for a radio;
television had not been
invented yet so there
was no talk getting to
them from the air or from
images on a screen
of the "Depression."

The sounds of the night
were crickets and frogs—
a robin singing, maybe,
a burro, occasionally,
or a goat's bell tinkling
as it shifted its location
in an enclosure with
the sheep; nothing urgent
or sad, just dogs barking,
announcing the time of
their watch— all pleasant
and comforting.

Wilfred bought a lot of
lumber for kitchen
cabinets and tables
and chairs he made
by himself.

Myrtle did the carving.

Then he tore into the ruin,
mixed mud mortar and
with adobe bricks, built
a fireplace to warm
chilly nights,

laid a flagstone floor—
and plastered up the holes
in the walls . . .

and did it look nice!

They planned an
additional room,
staked out the place
where it was to go—

mixed mud in a box,
added straw . . .

. . . and poured it into
a mold to make
adobe bricks;
let them lay in the sun
two days, stacked them
to further dry;

for building their
additional room . . .

which he built—
Myrtle helping;
then he plastered with mud,
inside and out.

After supper . . .

the moon came up—
and looked down with one big
round eye at all Wilfred and
Myrtle and their boys had done.

In the morning the cock crowed
and the goats woke up and
started to eat grass.

The chickens tried to steal
the apples from the pigs and
got their heads bitten off.

Wilfred plowed for a garden
to make ends meet—

Myrtle planted seeds.

And the boys played
in the dirt—
and in the ditch
that watered the garden
and the trees.

Things grew and grew.

The fruit trees
were so loaded
that the limbs had to
be propped up.

Myrtle began to pick.

Wilfred put the fruit
in a box or in baskets;

and a trucker
bought the lot—
(twelve hundred
bushels all told)

but— not counting
what they saved
to squeeze to make cider

or pare for the pot.

Wilfred cut alfalfa with a scythe;

Myrtle and Tommie wagoned it
to a place to cover it with a tarp.

Then Wilfred laid down
his tools and felt very
unhappy about what
the ranch had cost,
instead of made—

and painted a sign.

Myrtle (head in hand on
the edge of their bed)
began to worry and to think—
the move from the city was
her idea as well as his.

She cut her men's hair
to save—
and it added up
to quite a bit.

Wilfred helped the boys into their pajamas by the fire.

Myrtle took a bath in the washtub in the kitchen by the old black stove, with a candle placed near by.

Wilfred rocked in his chair
and puffed on his pipe
while Myrtle sat on the floor
until the fire went out.

They slept during the night—
and one morning
it began to snow.

Wilfred started drawings
for a book called
"Santa Fe Style Homes,
Charming and Practical"—

and the boys had
a snowball fight.

They butchered the pigs,
ate the chickens and
made a rug of the goat.

Then Myrtle took the axe—
and cut down the sign.

The artists, arm in arm,
agreed to leave the farming
to the farmers and to get
back to where they started—

to painting and to building
more adobe houses
on their ranch—

which has added several
more chapters to the story
of their life in the West—
all due to the "Depression"
and to an innocent little dream.

The End